The Odyss[...]

(It's a Really R[...]

Really Long Journey)

By Nina Segal

methuen | drama

LONDON • NEW YORK • OXFORD • NEW DELHI • SYDNEY

METHUEN DRAMA
Bloomsbury Publishing Plc
50 Bedford Square, London, WC1B 3DP, UK
1385 Broadway, New York, NY 10018, USA
29 Earlsfort Terrace, Dublin 2, Ireland

BLOOMSBURY, METHUEN DRAMA and the Methuen
Drama logo are trademarks of Bloomsbury Publishing Plc

First published in Great Britain 2024

A catalogue record for this book is available from the British Library.

A catalog record for this book is available from the Library of Congress.

ISBN: PB: 978-1-3504-5470-5
ePDF: 978-1-3504-5471-2
eBook: 978-1-3504-5472-9

Series: Plays for Young People

Typeset by Mark Heslington Ltd, Scarborough, North Yorkshire

To find out more about our authors and books visit
www.bloomsbury.com and sign up for our newsletters.

UNICORN

THE UK'S THEATRE FOR YOUNG AUDIENCES

The Odyssey
(It's a Really Really Really Long Journey)

By Nina Segal

This production of The Odyssey was produced by the Unicorn Theatre and opened in March 2024.

With special thanks to Molecule Theatre and the Royal Victoria Hall Foundation.

Supported using public funding by
ARTS COUNCIL
ENGLAND

Cast and Company

Muse	**Cerys Burton**
Muse	**Kimmy Edwards**
Penelope	**Cash Holland**
Telemachus	**Shaka Kalokoh**

Written by **Nina Segal**
Lyrics by **Nina Segal**
Music and Arrangements by **Naomi Hammerton**
Directed by **Jennifer Tang**
Set and Costume Design by **Rosie Elnile**
Choreography and Movement Direction by **Chi-San Howard**
Lighting Design by **Jessica Hung Han Yun**
Sound Design by **Eleanor Isherwood**
Video and Projection Design by **Virginie Taylor**
Casting Direction by **Chloe Blake**
Costume Supervisor **Isabelle Cook**
Musician and Music Producer **Pat Murdoch**

Production Manager **James Dawson**
Stage Manager **Lavinia Serban**
Deputy Stage Manager **Catherine Gibbs**

Assistant Stage Manager **Paris Wu**
Acting Assistant Stage Manager **Meredith Lewis**

Cerys Burton (Muse)

Cerys trained at Mountview Academy of Theatre Arts, graduating in 2022. Credits whilst training include: Paulette in *Legally Blonde*; Sarah in *Company*; Factory Girl in *Les Misérables*; Medium Alison in *Fun Home*; Sally Bowles in *Cabaret*. Other credits include: Soloist in *CDMT Event* (House of Commons); *Magic at the Musicals* (Royal Albert Hall).

Kimmy Edwards (Muse)

Kimmy trained at Guildford School of Acting. Theatre credits include: Ikette/Cover Tina in *One Night of Tina* (European tour); Emily Davison/Elsie Watkins/Cover Sylvia in *Sylvia* (The Old Vic); Cover Cindy Breakspeare in *Get Up Stand Up* (Lyric Theatre); Lois Lane/Bianca in *Kiss Me Kate* (Watermill Theatre); Michelle Morris/Cover Deena Jones in *Dreamgirls* (Savoy Theatre); Ensemble/Swing in *In the Heights* (King's Cross Theatre); Cover Felicia in *Memphis* (Shaftesbury Theatre); Ortisha in *Ghost the Musical* (UK tour); Dynamite in *Hairspray* (Germany); Acid Queen in *Tommy* (English Frankfurt Theatre/German tour); Judge/Saleswoman in *Legally Blonde* (Savoy Theatre).

Cash Holland (Penelope)

Cash trained at ArtsEd. Theatre credits include: *A Streetcar Named Desire* (Phoenix Theatre), *Julius Caesar* (Shakespeare's Globe), *Homos or Everyone in America* (Finborough Theatre).

Screen credits include: *Red Eye* (ITV), *The Completely Made-Up Adventures of Dick Turpin* (Apple TV+), *Out of Her Mind* (BBC Two).

Shaka Kalokoh (Telemachus)

Shaka trained at Guildhall School of Music and Drama, graduating in 2020. Recent theatre credits include: *Henry V*: schools tour (with the Donmar Warehouse) and *The Lion the*

Witch and the Wardrobe (Gillian Lynne Theatre). Shaka has collaborated with the Unicorn on a number of projects including *Marvin's Binoculars*.

CREATIVE TEAM

Nina Segal
Writer

Nina is a playwright and screenwriter. She was the recipient of the 2022 Playwright's Scheme Award and was shortlisted for the 2020 George Devine Award. Her first play *In the Night Time (Before the Sun Rises)* opened at the Gate Theatre to critical acclaim and subsequently had productions across Europe. She is currently under commission to Dutch National Opera and the RSC. In 2023, Nina's translation of *The Good Person of Szechwan* was performed at the Lyric Hammersmith and her original play *Shooting Hedda Gabler* opened at the Rose Theatre, both of which received excellent reviews.

On screen, she has written for *The Crown* and *Hanna*. Her short film *Capture* for the Financial Times has been acclaimed for giving an insight into the issue of online harm to young people and has run alongside debate around the online safety bill.

Naomi Hammerton
Music and Arrangements

Naomi is a composer, singer and conductor, and her songwriting spans genres; she writes and composes music for theatre, most recently working with the National Theatre and The PappyShow. She has written songs for and collaborated with multiple recording artists including Ray Davies (The Kinks), Jacob Collier, Alfie Boe and hotly tipped newcomer Leo. Recently she was honoured to accept a commission by Great Ormond Street Hospital to compose a piece of music to commemorate the closing of the Frontage

Building. Naomi has toured the world performing at multiple iconic venues and events including Glastonbury, Reading, Leeds and the Dubai Opera House. She has recently performed with the London Symphony Orchestra and London Voices recording scores for *The Guardians of the Galaxy* score, *Trolls 2 and 3* and *Elvis*, among others.

She is the founder of three thriving community choirs who perform regularly across London and the South East. She has recently written choral arrangements for Louise Redknapp, Dan Gillespie Sells (The Feeling) and The Hoosiers.

Jennifer Tang
Director

Jennifer is an award-winning theatre maker and stage director, specialising in making new work and fusing theatre with music. She trained at the University of East Anglia, the Young Vic and on the National Theatre Studio directors course. She was Genesis Fellow/Associate Director at the Young Vic 2020–22 and resident director for *Tina: The Tina Turner Musical* at Aldwych Theatre.

As director recent work includes: *The Tempest* (Regent's Park Open Air Theatre and Unicorn Theatre); *Further than the Furthest Thing*, *AI*, *The New Tomorrow* (Young Vic); *Gwei Miu/Ghost Girl* (Camden People's Theatre); *Mountains* (Royal Exchange and national tour); *We Are You* (Young Vic, British Museum); *Clytemnestra* (Gate Theatre); *Wanted* (West Yorkshire Playhouse) and *Constellations* and *One Day When We Were Young* (GEST, Sweden). Forthcoming/in development: *Bindweed* (Mercury Theatre, Colchester); *Twine* (Selina Thompson); *Fundamental* (NDT); and *Ghost Girl* for TV.

As assistant/associate director selected work includes: *Imperium*, *Snow in Midsummer* (RSC); *The Weaklings* (national tour); *The Edge of Our Bodies* (Gate Theatre); *Madman*, *Solid Air*, *Inside Wagner's Head* (The Drum, Plymouth);

#AIWEIWEI (Hampstead Theatre); and *The Owl and the Pussycat* (Royal Opera House).

Rosie Elnile
Set and Costume Designer

Rosie is an award-winning performance designer. She was a recipient of the Jerwood Live Work Fund 2020 and was an associate artist of the Gate Theatre.

Recent theatre credits include: *The Cherry Orchard, An Unfinished Man, Big Guns* (Yard Theatre); *Faggots and Their Friends between the Revolutions* (Manchester International Festival and Festival d'Aix-en-Provence); *Jason Medea Medley* (Staatsschauspiel, Dresden); *Titus Andronicus* (Shakespeare's Globe); *Sound of the Underground, A Fight Against... (Una Lucha Contra...), Goats, Primetime 2017* (Royal Court Theatre); *Paradise Now!* (Bush Theatre); *Violet* (Britten Pears Arts), co-production with Royal Opera and Music Theatre Wales; *Peaceophobia* (Fuel Theatre); *Prayer, The Ridiculous Darkness, The Unknown Island, The Convert* (Gate Theatre); *Thirst Trap* (Fuel Theatre); *Run Sister Run* (Crucible Theatre); *[Blank]* (Donmar Warehouse); *Our Town* (Regent's Park Open Air Theatre); *The Wolves* (Theatre Royal Stratford East); *The Mysteries, Three Sisters* (Royal Exchange Theatre); *Abandon* (Lyric Hammersmith); and *Returning to Haifa* (Finborough Theatre).

Chi-San Howard
Choreographer and Movement Director

Theatre credits include: *The Jungle Book, Never Have I Ever, The Narcissist, The Taxidermist's Daughter* (Chichester Festival Theatre); *A Little Princess* (Theatre by the Lake); *Grenfell: In the Words of Survivors* (National Theatre); *The Pillowman* (Duke of York's Theatre); *The Curious Case of Benjamin Button* (Southwark Playhouse Elephant); *Private Lives* (Donmar Warehouse); *Faun* (Cardboard Citizens/Theatre503);

Beginning, Glee and Me (Royal Exchange); *Les Misérables* (Sondheim Theatre, UK tour, Netherlands/Belgium tour); *Betty! A Sort of Musical* (Royal Exchange); *O, Island* (Royal Shakespeare Company); *Ivy Tiller: Vicar's Daughter, Squirrel Killer* (Royal Shakespeare Company); *A Midsummer Night's Dream* (Shakespeare North/Northern Stage); *Chasing Hares* (Young Vic); *That Is Not Who I Am/Rapture* (Royal Court); *Corrina, Corrina* (Headlong/Liverpool Everyman); *Anna Karenina* (Sheffield Crucible); *Two Billion Beats* (Orange Tree Theatre); *Aladdin* (Lyric Hammersmith); *Milk and Gall* (Theatre503); *Arrival* (Impossible Productions); *Typical Girls* (Clean Break/Sheffield Crucible); *Just So* (Watermill Theatre); *Home, I'm Darling* (Theatre by the Lake/Bolton Octagon/Stephen Joseph Theatre); *Harm* (Bush Theatre); *Living Newspaper Edition 5* (Royal Court); *Sunnymeade Court* (Defibrillator Theatre); *The Effect* (English Theatre Frankfurt); *The Sugar Syndrome* (Orange Tree Theatre); *Oor Wullie* (Dundee Rep/national tour); *Variations* (Dorfman Theatre/NT Connections); *Skellig* (Nottingham Playhouse); *Under the Umbrella* (Belgrade Theatre/Yellow Earth/ Tamasha); *Describe the Night* (Hampstead Theatre); *Fairytale Revolution, In Event of Moone Disaster* (Theatre503); *Cosmic Scallies* (Royal Exchange Manchester/Graeae); *Moth* (Hope Mill Theatre); *The Curious Case of Benjamin Button, Scarlet, The Tempest* (Southwark Playhouse); *Homos, or Everyone in America, Bury the Dead, Adding Machine: A Musical* (Finborough Theatre).

Film credits include: *Hurt by Paradise* (Sulk Youth Films); *Pretending* – Orla Gartland Music Video (Spindle); *I Wonder Why* – Joesef Music Video (Spindle); *Birds of Paradise* (Pemberton Films).

Jessica Hung Han Yun
Lighting Designer

Theatre credits include: *The Enormous Crocodile* (Leeds Playhouse/Regent's Park Open Air Theatre); *Minority Report*

(Nottingham Playhouse/Birmingham Rep/Lyric Hammersmith); *Lyonesse* (Harold Pinter Theatre); *Miss Saigon*, *The Good Person of Szechwan* (Sheffield Crucible); *Once on This Island* (Regent's Park Open Air Theatre); *My Neighbour Totoro* (RSC/Barbican); *Straight Line Crazy* (Bridge Theatre/The Shed, New York); *The Glow*, *Seven Methods of Killing Kylie Jenner* (also Public Theater, New York/Woolly Mammoth, Washington, DC); *Living Newspaper Edition 7*, *Pah-La* (Royal Court); *The Mirror and the Light* (RSC/Gielgud Theatre); *Anna X* (Lowry/Harold Pinter Theatre); *Marys Seacole*, *Blindness* (Donmar Warehouse); *Out West* (Lyric Hammersmith); *Inside* (Orange Tree Theatre); *The Band Plays On*, *She Loves Me* (Sheffield Theatres); *Dick Whittington* (National Theatre); *Rockets and Blue Lights* (Royal Exchange Manchester); *Faces in the Crowd*, *Mephisto*, *Dear Elizabeth*, *The Human Voice* (The Gate); *Equus* (Theatre Royal Stratford East/ETT/Trafalgar Studios/UK tour); *Armadillo* (Yard Theatre); *Reason to Stay Alive* (Sheffield Theatres/ETT/UK tour); *One* (Home/UK tour/international tour); *Forgotten* (Moongate/New Earth/Arcola Theatre/Theatre Royal Plymouth); *Hive City Legacy* (Hot Brown Honey/ Roundhouse). Dance credits include: *HOME* (Rambert2); *Twice-Born* (Scottish Ballet). Other credits include *DIVA* exhibition (V&A); *Guardians of the Galaxy: The Live Immersive Experience* (Secret Cinema); *Winter Light* (commissioned by the Museum of Home).

Jessica has won the Olivier Award and WhatsOnStage Award for Best Lighting for *My Neighbour Totoro,* the Knight of Illumination Award for Plays and Off West End Award for Best Lighting Design for *Equus*.

Eleanor Isherwood
Sound Designer

Ellie is a sound designer, composer, actor/musician and synth-pop artist (BYFYN). Her 'quietly ground breaking' work spans a vast array of forms, from site-specific theatre to binaural audio experiences. Recent work includes the composition and sound design for the new musical *The Light Princess*.

Virginie Taylor
Video and Projection Designer

Virginie is a London-based theatre video designer, with a background in lighting design and fine art. Her artistic journey is fuelled by a passion for devised theatre, new writing and politically engaged fringe shows. With an experimental approach to video design, she often blends analogue and digital techniques. She graduated from the Royal Central School of Speech and Drama, and Central Saint Martins in London. Virginie is now a visiting lecturer at the Royal Central School of Speech and Drama.

Recent video design credits include: *I'm Sorry I'm Not Lucy Liu* (Camden People's Theatre); *waiting for a train at the bus stop* (EdFringe); *Hummingbird* (VAULT Festival); *Press* (Park Theatre); *Charlie Russell Aims to Please* (EdFringe/The Other Palace); and *No Place Like Home* (EdFringe/Camden People's Theatre; 2022 LET Award winner). Recent lighting design credits include: *Storm* (Southwark Playhouse); *GIRLS* (The Old Market and *E-Man-A* (The Cockpit).

Chloe Blake
Casting Director

Theatre credits at the National Theatre include *Jekyll and Hyde* (schools tour), *Barrier(s)* and *Hamlet* (schools tour) as casting director; *Nye*, *The Effect*, *Blues for an Alabama Sky* as casting associate; *Standing at the Sky's Edge*, *Till the Stars Come Down* and *Small Island* as children's casting director; *Kerry Jackson* as additional casting. Further theatre credits include *The Wolf, the Duck and the Mouse* and *The Three Billy Goats Gruff* (Unicorn Theatre). As a freelance casting director credits include *Warehouse* (for theatre); *Satisfaction* (for screen); *Pull the Door* (for radio).

Unicorn Theatre

Transforming young lives through theatre.

At the Unicorn we create new, inventive and enthralling theatre experiences for children aged up to 13. Every year, we welcome around 65,000 families and schools through our doors, and many thousands more through Unicorn Online.

We believe that young people of all ages, perspectives and abilities have the right to experience exciting, entertaining and inspiring work and we actively seek out children who wouldn't otherwise attend, offering free tickets where needed.

We develop work with children from our partner schools and community groups to ensure that our work remains relevant and informed by the young people we serve. Our values of courage, curiosity and respect run through everything we do.

The Odyssey
(It's a Really Really Really Long Journey)

For Hart and Ted

My heart, my bones, my joy, my world.

This is a play for four performers.

The first plays **Telemachus**, *a young boy.*

The second plays **Penelope**, *his mother; also* **Cyclops**, **Calypso**, **Circe**, **Tiresias** *and* **Scylla**.

The third and fourth play the Muses, taking on the roles of **Ithacans**, **Trojans**, **Sheep**, **Sirens**, **Wild Beasts** *and* **Guards**.

One: Ithaca

Music begins. The **Ithacans** *and* **Penelope** – *in matching outfits, with elaborate beehive hairdos – perform in front of a glitter curtain. They sing.*

Penelope
It starts – like many stories – with a man.
A man leaving – heard that before?
A man going off to find his fortune.
A man going off to start a war.

Ithacans
It starts – with a child.
A baby boy who's left behind.
And a woman, of course.
Someone has to stay by that boy's side.

Penelope
And the years go past and the boy grows up,
Until he's almost grown.
He starts to wonder where his dad is,
And when it is he's coming home.

Ithacans
And the woman –
Well, she's been wondering the very same.
But you don't talk about these things with children.
It's not the kind of thing that's easy to explain.

Penelope
What's there to say – your father's gone,
Went off to fight a war in Troy.
He went to help his friend out,
And he left behind a baby boy.

Ithacans
Now all his friends are back or dead.
Returned or turned divine.
But her man, his father, Odysseus –
There are rumours, but there's no sign.

Penelope
Some people say that he was lost in battle,
Some people say that he was lost at sea,
Some people say he's lost his senses,
Some people say that he'll be home for tea.

Ithacans
But she doesn't listen to the rumours,
She prefers to hear the music instead.
If the world gets too loud, you can drown it all out,
With a song that you keep in your head,
And the song goes –

The **Ithacans** *harmonise behind her, as* **Penelope** *dances – for a moment, carefree. Then –* **Telemachus** *enters.*

Telemachus   Mum!

The music cuts out, as **Penelope** *turns to see a mortified* **Telemachus**.

Telemachus   What are you doing?

Penelope   I'm dancing –

Telemachus   Why?

Penelope   Why not?

Telemachus   Because it's embarrassing –

Penelope   Why's it embarrassing?

Telemachus   Because you're my mum. And because you're meant to be in mourning. For dad.

Penelope   Honey, your dad's not dead –

Telemachus   How do you know?

Penelope   I have to believe that he's still living – he's out there, trying to get home. And until he does –

Telemachus   You'll be here dancing.

He scowls. **Penelope** *sighs – then picks up her sewing.*

Telemachus   Dancing and sewing.

Penelope   Do you think I sew for fun?

Telemachus   It doesn't look like fun –

Penelope   It's not – but I have to do it.

Telemachus   Why? Because you need a new –

He reaches for **Penelope***'s sewing, before she can stop him.*

Telemachus   Wedding dress? But you don't need a wedding dress –

Penelope   No, I don't –

Telemachus   So why are you sewing a wedding dress? Mum?

He waits for an answer. **Penelope** *hesitates – then, falteringly:*

Penelope   There are some people – men – who think the same as you. My husband has been gone so long – he must be dead. And so –

Telemachus   You're going to marry someone else?

Penelope   I'm not –

Telemachus   So why do you need a wedding dress?

Penelope   I don't, I just need – time. That's what this is – it's time.

Telemachus   It doesn't look like time – looks like a wedding dress –

Penelope   Each day I sew – and every night undo the whole day's work. This dress will always be unfinished – so there will be no wedding day.

Telemachus   Why don't you just say no?

Penelope   Not every man will listen when a woman tells him no. So I pretend –

Telemachus   You lie.

Penelope   I don't want to –

Telemachus   But you do.

Penelope   What else can I do? I can't fight, I can't leave –

Telemachus   Why not?

Telemachus *turns to exit.* **Penelope** *calls after him:*

Penelope   Where are you going?

Telemachus   I'm not waiting anymore. I'm going to find my dad.

Penelope   But he left years ago, he could be anywhere –

Telemachus   You said he went to Troy – so I'll start in Troy.

Penelope   You can't go to Troy, you're a child –

Telemachus   I'm his child – and he needs my help.

Penelope   He's an adult, he can look after himself –

Telemachus   What about looking after me? He should be here.

Penelope   He should be – but he's not. And I don't find that easy either – but I do my best. I have been doing my best. For years. For you. And I don't think you understand how hard that's been. How hard that is. The things I do –

Telemachus   Like lying? Dancing and sewing and lying –

Penelope *interrupts* **Telemachus** *with a shout of frustration – sudden, loud, almost monstrous. He shrinks away, frightened. She takes a breath.*

Penelope   I'm sorry – I didn't mean to shout at you. But all this talk of leaving – it reminds me of your father –

Telemachus   It's not a bad thing, to be like Dad.

Penelope   It's not. And you're like him – you are. So much that sometimes –

She stops, unable to continue. She takes a moment, then:

Penelope   I know your dad would be here if he could –

Telemachus   How do you know?

Penelope   Because he loves you –

Telemachus   Then why hasn't he come home?

Penelope   It's – complicated. There could be lots of reasons.

Telemachus   I wish grown-ups would say when they don't know.

Penelope   Telemachus, please – I can't let you go –

Telemachus   Actually, you can't stop me. I'm not a kid anymore.

He exits – **Penelope** *follows him. The music returns.*

First Ithacan
 People say Telemachus is leaving.
 People say that he's going to Troy.

Second Ithacan
 People say – oh my God, he can't do that!
 Telemachus – he's just a young boy.

Telemachus *returns, carrying a wooden sword.*

Telemachus   I said – I'm not a kid anymore!

First Ithacan
 Telemachus says he won't be staying,
 Telemachus says he's got to go.

Second Ithacan
 Telemachus says he's off on his own,
 But Penelope, she says –

Penelope *enters, carrying a backpack.*

Penelope   No!

First Ithacan
    Penelope says he's too young to leave her –

Penelope   Go alone? It's too much to bear –

Telemachus   Fine, then someone can come with me –

Penelope *looks at the* **Ithacans***, pleadingly – but they look unconvinced.*

Ithacans
    Us? But we'd rather stay here.

Second Ithacan
    We've heard Troy's pretty dangerous –
    They had a big war there, you know?

Telemachus
    But that war is many years over –
    And my father still hasn't come home.

Penelope
    If the boy is determined to find him,
    Then how can I force him to stay?
    After all, I'm only his mother –
    He won't listen, whatever I say.

    But if you would agree to go with him,
    Then I'd know that my son's not alone.
    And if you find my husband, he owes me a call –
    I'll be waiting at home by the phone.

Telemachus *hands swords to the* **Ithacans***. They accept, begrudgingly.*

Ithacans
    Telemachus says we're really leaving –

Second Ithacan
    We're going and we don't know
    When we'll be back –

Telemachus   Wallet, shoes, keys, sword – what else?

Penelope *folds a letter, placing it in the backpack.*

Penelope   Your backpack.

She hands **Telemachus** *the backpack. He hugs her tightly.*

Telemachus
I'll come home when I've got what I set out to find.

Penelope
Just come home whenever – come home anytime.
The door's always open, the phone's always on,
Just promise you won't be too long.

Telemachus
I'll be back, Mum, as soon as
I've done what I need,
When I've tracked down my dad,
And brought him home with me.
Then you'll get your son back,
And your husband too –

Penelope
I pray that's not too good to be true.

Telemachus   Bye, Mum – love you –

Penelope   Love you too.

She hugs **Telemachus**. *As he exits with the* **Ithacans**, *she sings:*

Penelope
Pray that he won't be lost to me in battle,
Pray that he won't be lost to me at sea,
Pray he will keep hold of his senses,
Pray that he'll be home in time for tea.

I can't think about all that could happen –
So I'll listen to the music instead.
If the world gets too loud, you can drown it all out,
With a song that you keep in your head,
And the song goes –

The music rises once more – **Penelope** *tries to dance, but falters. She exits, rushing clumsily off the stage – as the music continues.*

Two: Troy

Telemachus *enters with the* **Ithacans**. *He hesitates at the water's edge.*

First Ithacan   You okay?

Telemachus   Yeah, fine. Just – never been in a boat before.

Second Ithacan   First time leaving Ithaca?

Telemachus   First time leaving home.

First Ithacan   We could go back. We can still do that.

Telemachus   No – I need to do this.

Second Ithacan   Okay – ready?

Telemachus   Ready.

He and the **Ithacans** *step into the boat. A moment, then:*

Telemachus   How long does it takes to get to Troy?

First Ithacan   We've been in the boat for less than one minute.

Telemachus   I'm hungry – did we bring snacks? We must have brought snacks. What's in the bag?

The **First Ithacan** *opens the backpack. She pulls out a piece of paper.*

First Ithacan   There's a note here – from your mum. Says she's packed everything you might need for an odyssey.

Telemachus   A what?

Second Ithacan   A really really really long journey.

Telemachus   How long?

Second Ithacan   Really really really long.

Telemachus   If it's that long, then there must be snacks.

The **First Ithacan** *reaches into the backpack – and pulls out headphones.*

First Ithacan   Headphones –

Telemachus   Not a snack.

The **Second Ithacan** *reaches into the backpack – and pulls out a rope.*

Second Ithacan   A rope –

Telemachus   I can't eat that.

The **First Ithacan** *reaches into the backpack – and pulls out a rabbit.*

First Ithacan   A fluffy bunny –

Second Ithacan   Technically edible –

Telemachus   No, he's not. He's Roger – and he's very special.

He takes the rabbit, cuddling it. The **Second Ithacan** *reaches into the backpack – and pulls out a letter.*

Second Ithacan   And there's a letter here. It's sealed.

Telemachus   Should we open it?

Second Ithacan   It says 'don't open, until you really need to'.

Telemachus   Does it look like it has food in it?

Second Ithacan   It looks like a letter.

Telemachus   Then we don't need it. What else?

The **First Ithacan** *reaches into the backpack – and pulls out a photo.*

First Ithacan   There's a photo – of a baby and a man.

Second Ithacan   A handsome man.

Telemachus   He isn't handsome – he's my dad.

Second Ithacan   Dads can be handsome. Normally someone has to find them handsome for them to even be a dad.

First Ithacan   Aw, that's you? That little baby?

Telemachus   No. I mean, yeah. But not anymore. I'm big now. And strong. And hungry. Let me look in the bag.

He takes the bag. His face lights up, as he pulls out a cake.

Cake!

Second Ithacan   There's cake?

Telemachus   Let's eat the cake!

First Ithacan   Wait –

Second Ithacan   Don't wait! Cake!

First Ithacan   But it could be weeks until we get to Troy –

The boat lurches, as they reach land. **Telemachus** *and the* **Ithacans** *are thrown from the boat, landing on the shore. They look around, disorientated.*

Second Ithacan   Troy!

Telemachus   Are you sure? I thought Troy was a major city –

First Ithacan   It was – but then they had a war.

Second Ithacan   It's a shame, really – a great city like Troy, destroyed. By your dad.

Telemachus   He didn't destroy it –

Second Ithacan   Look around – I think he did.

Telemachus   Are we here to find him or be mean about him?

First Ithacan   We're here to find him –

Telemachus   Right. So – find him. I'll stay here to guard the boat –

Second Ithacan   You're not just trying to make us leave so you can eat the cake?

Telemachus   Of course I'm not – I'm going to guard the cake.

*The **Ithacans** hesitate, then exit. **Telemachus** unwraps the cake.*

Telemachus   Time to guard you in my stomach!

*Before he takes a bite, the **Trojans** enter.*

First Trojan   You, stranger – what's your business here?

Telemachus   I come in peace –

Second Trojan   That's what they all say – that they come in peace.

First Trojan   Next thing you know? No peace!

Second Trojan   The last time strangers landed boats upon our shore, they burned our city to the ground.

First Trojan   Destroyed it! Those unruly Ithacans!

*The **Second Trojan** spits at the **First Trojan**'s mention of the Ithacans.*

Second Trojan   I hate to even hear the name! Ithacans!

*The **First Trojan** spits at the **Second Trojan**'s mention of the Ithacans.*

First Trojan   Ithacans!

*Before the **Trojans** can spit again, **Telemachus** interrupts.*

Telemachus   You know they aren't all bad, the Ithacans –

*Both **Trojans** spit at **Telemachus**' mention of the Ithacans. Then:*

First Trojan   Are you not listening? They burned our city down!

Telemachus   I'm sure they didn't do it on purpose –

Second Trojan   You think you burn a city down by accident? No, they wanted to do it – waited ten long years for it –

Telemachus   Ten years?

Trojans   Ten years.

First Trojan   No more, no less –

Trojans   Ten years.

Music begins. The **Trojans** *sing.*

Second Trojan
Ten years, they held our city under siege.
Did what they could to bring us to our knees.
We locked the gates to keep the wolves at bay,
And yet –

Telemachus
They got in anyway?

Trojans
They got in anyway!

First Trojan
Their actions took an unexpected course,
The winning plan involved –

Second Trojan
You'll never guess –

Trojans
A horse!

First Trojan
We woke one morning to a wondrous sight –

Trojans
The Ithacans had left the previous night!

Second Trojan
  And in their place, there stood a wooden horse –

First Trojan
  We brought it right inside, of course!

Trojans
  Soon as it got past the gates,
  They left their horsey hiding place.
  They massacred the lot of us –
  Those Ithacans and their Odysseus.

Telemachus
  Odysseus? You know him then?

First Trojan
  Enough to know the man is bad –

Second Trojan
  You've met him too, have you?

Telemachus
  Odysseus – he is my dad.

The music suddenly stops. Tension. **Telemachus** *shifts, awkwardly.*

First Trojan   You know – I don't like to speak ill of anyone's father. But your dad caused a lot of damage here.

Telemachus   I'm sure he didn't mean to –

Second Trojan   Whether he intended to or not – he did. He came. He saw. He sacked our city.

Telemachus   And then? What happened next?

First Trojan   We salvaged what we could and carried on –

Telemachus   I mean what happened to my dad –

Second Trojan   He left. Once there was nothing more to turn to rubble – off he went.

Telemachus   Do you know where?

First Trojan   Towards the cyclops' cave.

Telemachus   The what?

Second Trojan   It's a cave, belonging to a cyclops.

Telemachus   A cyclops?

First Trojan   Yes! How many times!

Telemachus   I have to go into a cyclops' cave?

Second Trojan   Nobody said you have to go –

Telemachus   That's where my dad went, so I'll follow him –

First Trojan   Like father, like son –

Second Trojan   Both fools!

The **Trojans** *shake their heads – as* **Telemachus** *exits.*

Three: The Cyclops

Telemachus *enters – sword raised, body tense. He walks, cautiously.*

Telemachus   Okay – you're looking for a cave. A cyclops' cave. A cyclops is a monster. A giant one-eyed monster. Who eats people. And you're looking for his cave.

He suddenly stops – a realisation.

What am I doing? This isn't what I do.

For a moment, it seems like he's about to turn and run. Then:

But it is what my dad does. He went into the cyclops' cave. He didn't turn and run away. And I'm his son – so I can do it too. Even if I really really really don't want to.

He hesitates – then charges forward, sword swinging, eyes closed. Two **Sheep** *appear out of the dark. As* **Telemachus** *approaches:*

First Sheep   Woah, woah, woah –

Second Sheep   Watch where you're swinging that thing –

First Sheep   I'm not due a shearing for a month.

Telemachus   Hold on – you're not a cyclops –

First Sheep   No, I'm not. A cyclops? Me?

Second Sheep   You thought she was a cyclops?

First Sheep   Two eyes, four legs, woolly coat –

Telemachus   You're a sheep.

Second Sheep   The boy's a genius.

Telemachus   But I thought this was the cyclops' cave?

First Sheep   Cyclops' cave, that way – though I would steer well clear, if I were you. No man goes in and comes back out – not in one piece, anyway!

The **Sheep** *laugh.* **Telemachus** *looks horrified.*

Second Sheep   Sorry, that's funny to us because we're not men – but if we were men, it would probably seem quite horrifying. You do look quite horrified, actually.

Telemachus   My dad went into the cyclops' cave.

Second Sheep   And did he come back out? In one piece or –

First Sheep   Look, I don't want to be the bearer of bad news – but I would say your dad has probably been one hundred per cent eaten by a cyclops.

The **Second Sheep** *laughs again.*

Second Sheep   Sorry – I'm not laughing at your dad being eaten by a cyclops – God, why would I laugh at that?

Telemachus   So why are you laughing?

Second Sheep   Because she said 'bearer'. Bearer of bad news? And we're sheep. So we go 'baa'. So she's the 'baa-er of bad news'. You get it? Do you get it?

Telemachus   You're telling me my dad's been eaten by a cyclops –

Second Sheep   That's the bad news she's 'baa-ing'!

*The **Sheep** fall about laughing. The **Cyclops'** voice is heard from offstage:*

Cyclops   Who goes there? This is the cyclops' cave –

Telemachus   Who's that?

First Sheep   The cyclops! Quick – pretend to be a sheep –

Telemachus   I'm nothing like a sheep –

First Sheep   A shame, for you. But it's your only chance of getting out alive. So – sheep.

*The **Sheep** conceal **Telemachus** between them, as he assumes his best impression of a sheep. The **Cyclops** enters.*

Cyclops   Who's there?

Second Sheep   It's just your sheep –

Telemachus   Just three completely normal sheep.

*The **Cyclops** approaches the **Sheep**. He stops at **Telemachus**.*

Cyclops   You're not a normal sheep –

Telemachus   I – am –

Cyclops   No sheep is normal – every sheep is special, every one of you. That's what we say, isn't it?

Sheep   Every sheep is special.

Telemachus   Is that what we say?

Cyclops   You must be new –

Telemachus   I am. A new sheep. But definitely a sheep.

Cyclops   Let's get you settled in – come on, inside –

Telemachus   But I don't want to go inside –

The **Cyclops** *herds* **Telemachus** *and the* **Sheep** *inside –*
Telemachus *watches in horror as the cave entrance closes*
behind him. Music begins. The **Cyclops** *and* **Telemachus** *sing*
or speak over it.

Cyclops
  Go on now, make yourself at home –

Telemachus
  I really would prefer to roam –

Cyclops
  But in here, you'll be nice and safe –

Telemachus
  Be safe? Inside the cyclops' cave?

Cyclops
  Believe me, there's no need to fear –
  I wouldn't harm a sheep, my dear.
  You sheep have personalities,
  Have souls, ambitions, special dreams –

Telemachus
  And yet you trap us in your cave –

Cyclops
  I'm only trying, dear, to keep you safe.
  And I do let you out to graze –
  At least two or three times a day.

Telemachus
  Apart from that, the cave is locked?

Cyclops
  By an extremely heavy rock.
  You have to be protected, see –

Telemachus
  From who?

Cyclops
  From men, those vicious beasts.

Telemachus
Are men so bad?

Cyclops
Oh, abso-lu-te-ly.
Most men have no humanity –
So I devour them guilt-free.

Telemachus
It's true – you really do eat men –

Cyclops
He seems confused, your friend –

First Sheep
Be careful or he'll find you out –

Second Sheep
The more you ask, the more he'll doubt.

Telemachus
And if he finds out I'm a man?

Second Sheep
You'd better have a clever plan.

Telemachus *turns to the* **Cyclops**. *With an air of faux-nonchalance:*

Telemachus
Cyclops – a question –

Cyclops
Yes, my dear?

Telemachus
Has any man escaped from here?

Cyclops
There was one, many years ago –
Odysseus – my greatest foe.

Telemachus
Odysseus? My dad got free!

Cyclops
   Your dad? But your dad was a sheep –

Suspicious, the **Cyclops** *takes a closer look at* **Telemachus***. He sniffs him. Maybe he even has a taste. Then his single eye widens – a realisation.*

Cyclops
   Hold on, I recognise that taste –
   Waiter – bring the plates!

Telemachus *tries desperately to escape, as the* **Cyclops** *salivates.*

Telemachus
   No, please – I'm just a boy –
   A meal of me won't bring much joy.
   There'll be much more of me, you know,
   If you can wait until I grow.

The music stops. The **Cyclops** *eyes* **Telemachus** *warily.*

Cyclops   But how long is that going to take?

Telemachus   It could be years –

Cyclops   And what are we going to do in the meantime?

Telemachus   We could – tell stories –

Cyclops   About what?

Telemachus   About – my dad.

Cyclops   This isn't some kind of clever plan, is it?

Telemachus   Of course not. I just – never knew my dad. So if you could tell me anything – it would mean a lot –

Cyclops   I never knew my dad either. I mean, I knew him – but I didn't really know him.

Telemachus   What was he like?

Cyclops   He was a cyclops. Like me. But we were – very different. He never really understood me. He used to tell me – 'Son, your friendship with these sheep, it isn't right, it isn't natural –'

Telemachus   Cyclops –

Cyclops   Yes?

Telemachus   I – was asking you about my dad?

Cyclops   Of course – your dad. Let's see. He was a clever man. Cunning. Too cunning.

Telemachus   He tricked you?

Cyclops   Nobody can trick me! But, yes – he tricked me.

Telemachus   How?

Cyclops   You think I'm going to tell you? So you can follow in his footsteps and escape yourself? Good luck with that – nobody tricks me twice! Since that day forward, I've made sure to keep no rope in here –

Telemachus *glances towards his backpack – the rope is visible.*

Telemachus   That's how he escaped? He used a rope?

Cyclops   He did – but like I say, I won't be fooled a second time. I've got my eye on you – and I won't be distracted –

Telemachus   Not even – with a song?

Music begins. The **Cyclops** *turns away from* **Telemachus**, *towards it.*

Cyclops   Oh, go on then!

As the **Cyclops** *sings or speaks, distracted by the music,* **Telemachus** *quietly retrieves the rope from his backpack.*

Cyclops
   Your father was a clever man –
   And so he hatched a clever plan.
   He tied himself onto a sheep,
   Disguised himself within its fleece.

As the **Cyclops** *continues,* **Telemachus** *ties himself onto a* **Sheep**.

Cyclops
  And when I let them out to graze,
  Cunning Odysseus escaped.
  But since that day I've made quite sure,
  To keep no rope in here at all.

Disguised within the **Sheep**'s *fleece,* **Telemachus** *puts on a*
Sheep *voice:*

Telemachus   Cyclops, talking of grazing –

Cyclops   Oh, is it time already? Here you go –

The **Cyclops** *removes the rock from the entrance, to let the*
Sheep *out.*

Cyclops   Now – where was I?

As **Telemachus** *escapes the cave, hidden with the* **Sheep**'s *fleece,*
the **Cyclops** *continues singing, his song reaching its crescendo:*

Cyclops
  Yes, there's no hope of breaking loose,
  For you will find no rope to use!
  There's no way to escape my den –
  This cyclops won't be fooled again!

The **Cyclops** *turns, expecting to see* **Telemachus** *– but he is gone.*

Cyclops   Hello?

The **Cyclops**' *voice echoes – he is alone. The music rises, as a glitter*
curtain falls.

Cyclops
  Again the silence descends –
  Find myself alone again.
  Now that the child has gone,
  It will be dinner for one.

Behind the **Cyclops** *the* **Sheep** *re-enter, singing backing vocals.*

Cyclops
  Feel so hungry but I can't even eat –

Sheep
Without you –

Cyclops
Feel so empty that I can't even sleep –

Sheep
Without you –

Cyclops
All I dream of is to feel your heartbeat –

Sheep
But now he's gone –

Cyclops
This is a cave, not a home –

Sheep
You're all alone.

Cyclops
Now that the child is free,
No happy ending for little me.
Oh it's a lonely life,
You don't need two eyes to see.

As the **Sheep** *dance behind the* **Cyclops***, a mirror ball descends.*

Cyclops
Without the pitter-patter of tiny feet –

Sheep
Without you!

Cyclops
There's a hollow feeling growing in me –

Sheep
Without you!

Cyclops
I can't survive without the child here with me –

Sheep
But now he's gone –

Cyclops
And I'm alone!

Sheep
He's all alone!

The **Cyclops'** *costume falls away – his mask slipping, to reveal* **Penelope***.*

Penelope
Again the silence descends –
Find myself alone again.
Now that my child has gone,
It will be dinner for one.

The **Sheep** *have stopped dancing. They watch* **Penelope** *with concern.*

Penelope
Feel so hungry but I can't even eat –
Feel so tired but I can't even sleep –
All I dream of is to feel your heartbeat,
But now you're gone –
This is a cave, not a home.

Overcome, **Penelope** *exits, followed by the* **Sheep***.*

Four: The Lotus Eaters

Telemachus *enters, alone. Laughter, offstage – the* **Ithacans** *enter.*

Telemachus   There you are! Where've you been?

First Ithacan   Sorry – who are you?

The **Ithacans** *stare at* **Telemachus***, glassy-eyed. He frowns, frustrated.*

Telemachus   Telemachus? We sailed from Ithaca? You left me on the shore and I was set upon by Trojans? And a cyclops? And two talking sheep?

Second Ithacan   I don't think we've met before –

First Ithacan   I've never even heard of Ithaca –

Second Ithacan   Or talking sheep!

The **Ithacans** *laugh.* **Telemachus** *stares at them in disbelief.*

Telemachus   What's going on? Why are you acting like you don't remember me? Or Ithaca – your home –

First Ithacan   Our home?

Second Ithacan   This is our home – and it's paradise.

Telemachus *looks around, confused – it doesn't seem like paradise to him.*

Telemachus   You think this place is paradise?

Music as **Calypso** *appears from a grove of lotus trees. She sings.*

Calypso
　　Welcome to paradise!
　　Don't have to ask me twice –
　　Of course you're welcome here!
　　Come while away the day,
　　It's the Calypso way –
　　Can I get you a wine or a beer?

Telemachus   I don't drink beer –

Calypso   A smoothie then!

Calypso *hands* **Telemachus** *a colourful smoothie.*

Calypso
　　Made with the freshest fruit,
　　Blended up just for you –
　　Our smoothies make you dance and sing!

Ithacans
Dance and sing!

Calypso
Go on and have a taste,
A fruit you can't quite place,
Smoothies so good you forget everything!

Telemachus *is about to take a sip of smoothie – but stops himself.*

Telemachus   Sorry – what did you say?

Calypso   About how delicious the smoothies are?

Telemachus   About forgetting everything –

Calypso   Oh yes – our smoothies are made from the lotus plant, a local delicacy! Packed full of natural fruit sugars, the lotus plant is guaranteed to satisfy your appetite – and erase your memory!

Second Ithacan   You've really got to try it!

The **Second Ithacan** *takes a drink of smoothie – then repeats herself.*

Second Ithacan   You've really got to try it!

Calypso
With taste of summer fruits,
And just a hint of roots –
And bitter undertones.
Soon as it hits your tongue,
There's nothing can be done –
You will lose all thoughts of home!

Telemachus   Hold on – explain that again –

Calypso   Of course – so we use both the lotus flower and the roots, which gives the drink an earthier taste –

Telemachus   No – about losing all thoughts of home –

Calypso *and the* **Ithacans** *dance and sing around* **Telemachus.**

Calypso
> You forget every face,
> Shut out all other place,
> Notions of home will pass you by –

Ithacans
> Pass you by!

Calypso
> With just one sip of juice,
> Your memory you lose –
> So go on, darling, have a try!

Telemachus   No, thanks. I'm sure it's delicious –

Calypso   I assure you, it is –

Telemachus   But I know not to take gifts from strangers.

Calypso   And I'm a stranger, am I? That's easy to fix –

Calypso *reaches out to shake* **Telemachus'** *hand.*

Calypso   Calypso. Goddess.

Telemachus   You're a goddess?

Calypso   Obviously. And you are?

Telemachus   Telemachus.

Calypso   Nice to meet you. So, now we're not strangers anymore – drink up!

Telemachus   But I'm not sure I want to forget my home –

First Ithacan   You won't remember what you're missing!

The **First Ithacan** *takes a drink of smoothie – then repeats herself.*

First Ithacan   You won't remember what you're missing!

Telemachus   But I like my home – why would I want to forget it?

Calypso   If you like it so much, why did you leave?

Telemachus   I didn't want to leave – I had to. To find my dad.

Calypso   And you think he might be here, do you?

Telemachus   He might be. Maybe that's why he never came home – because he forgot he had one.

Calypso   What's his name, your dad?

Telemachus   Odysseus.

Calypso   Odysseus!

Telemachus   You know him?

Calypso   Know him? I fell in love with him – he's an extremely charming man, your father.

Telemachus   I might need some memory-erasing fruit, after all.

Calypso   Unfortunately for you – and me – he isn't here.

Telemachus   But he was?

Calypso   Yes – and it was paradise. But no matter how much fruit he ate or how many years passed, he never lost his thoughts of home. And so he left.

Telemachus   Where to?

Calypso   To Ithaca, he said. I gave him wind –

Telemachus   From too much fruit?

Calypso   Not wind – magic wind. A bag of it. Enough to get him safely home – as long as he only opened it the tiniest amount. Of course, if he opened the bag of wind more than the tiniest amount – he would be blown far from home.

Telemachus   But why would he have opened it up more than a tiny amount, if you had warned him not to?

Calypso   I'm a goddess – doesn't mean people listen to me.

Telemachus   And what direction did the wind blow him in?

Calypso   Only one way to find out –

Calypso *hands* **Telemachus** *a bag of wind, tied with silver thread.*

Calypso   I don't know how you'll convince your companions to go with you – they seem pretty happy here –

Telemachus   I think I might have something.

He reaches into his backpack – to get the cake. The **Ithacans** *reach for it, greedily.* **Telemachus** *grips their hands, then opens up the bag of wind – and they fly upwards together.*

Five: The Sirens

Telemachus *and the* **Ithacans** *float down to land on the stage. The sound of waves – they are at sea. The* **Ithacans** *rub their eyes groggily.*

First Ithacan   Where are we?

Second Ithacan   Who are we?

First Ithacan   What's happened in the last – three days?

Second Ithacan   Five days?

First Ithacan   I don't remember much –

Telemachus   I'm not surprised – you ate a lot of lotus fruit.

Second Ithacan   What's lotus fruit?

Telemachus   It takes away your memory. If you hadn't eaten it, you would remember that.

Second Ithacan   I don't remember anything – but I know you saved us. So – thanks.

Telemachus   I don't want you to thank me –

Second Ithacan   Okay, then – no thanks?

Telemachus   I don't want to be in situations where you have to thank me. You're meant to be the grown-ups – but it's always me that's looking after you.

First Ithacan   I thought you wanted to be the grown-up –

Telemachus   I said I didn't want to be a kid anymore – but maybe I was wrong. Maybe I shouldn't even be here. Maybe I should just give up – go home –

Second Ithacan   But what about finding your dad?

Telemachus   Maybe he doesn't want to be found. Calypso said he stayed with her for years – that doesn't sound like someone very interested in coming home.

First Ithacan   But if the lotus plant made him forget his home –

Telemachus   She said the plant had no effect on him – which means it was his choice to stay away. For years.

Telemachus *turns away from the* **Ithacans**, *as they exchange glances.*

Second Ithacan   Look – even adults make mistakes. You want them to be perfect, but they aren't –

Telemachus   So what's the point of them? Maybe I'm better off by myself – I always end up on my own anyway.

He moves to the edge of the boat, preparing to jump.

First Ithacan   Telemachus – we can't let you go –

Telemachus   You sound like my mum – but you're not my mum.

Before the **Ithacans** *can stop him,* **Telemachus** *jumps into the sea – when he resurfaces, they are gone. As he struggles against the waves:*

Telemachus
   I turn to look for the boat –
   I try, but I can't stay afloat.

Now that the grown-ups have gone,
I wonder – what have I done?

Telemachus *is pulled under the water. As he surfaces again:*

Telemachus
And I really miss my mum.

Penelope *enters, watching* **Telemachus**. *She sings, calling to him.*

Penelope
Feel so hungry but I can't even eat –

Telemachus   Mum?

Penelope
Feel so tired but I can't even sleep –

Telemachus   Mum!

Penelope
All I dream of is to feel your heartbeat –

As **Telemachus** *turns to see* **Penelope**, *she reaches out for him.*

Penelope   Telemachus!

Telemachus *gasps, then swallows water. He sinks. When he resurfaces,* **Penelope** *has turned away. Desperate, he swims to her.*

Telemachus   Mum? Mum!

He reaches **Penelope**. *She turns to him – but it isn't her anymore. It is a* **Siren**. **Telemachus** *backs away in horror.*

Telemachus   I'm sorry – I thought you were somebody else –

The **Siren** *sings –* **Telemachus** *is entranced.* **Penelope** *enters again.*

Penelope   Telemachus –

Telemachus   Mum?

He turns towards **Penelope** – *but she turns away once more. He swims towards her voice – but the figure is revealed as another* **Siren**.

Telemachus   You're not my mum –

The **Sirens** *harmonise –* **Telemachus** *is enchanted.* **Penelope** *enters.*

Penelope   Telemachus!

Telemachus *turns and swims towards* **Penelope** – *then stops, unsure.*

Telemachus   Mum? How can I trust it's you?

Penelope *and the* **Sirens** *continue singing, competing for* **Telemachus**' *attention.*

Sirens
     Don't think about all that could happen,
     Just listen to the music instead.
     With a head full of sound,
     You can swim till you drown,
     As life becomes death.
     And the song goes –

Penelope
     I can't think about all that could happen,
     Every ending but one simply fills me with dread.
     When my fears get too loud, I just drown it all out,
     With a song that I keep in my head –

As **Penelope** *continues singing, she grows increasingly desperate.*

Penelope
     Pray that you won't be lost to me in battle,
     Pray that you won't be lost to me at sea,
     Pray that you'll keep hold of your senses,
     Pray that you'll be home in time for tea.

Sirens
     Swim till you drown –

Penelope
    Drown it all out –

Telemachus, *overwhelmed, reaches into his backpack for the headphones. As he puts them on, the* **Sirens** *disappear – but* **Penelope** *begins to fade too. Torn,* **Telemachus** *removes the headphones.* **Penelope** *– and the* **Sirens** *– return.* **Penelope** *gestures desperately for* **Telemachus** *to put the headphones back on. He does – then collapses.*

Six: Circe

Telemachus, *sleeping, is transported – into a child's bedroom.* **Circe** *tucks him gently into bed. As he sleeps, she sings.*

Circe
    It starts – with a child.
    A baby boy who has left his home.
    He starts to understand how big the world is –
    And what it is to move through it alone.

    And he's brave and strong and he tries his best,
    But he isn't built to fight.
    He wants to follow in his father's footsteps –
    But still needs comfort in the night.

Circe *opens* **Telemachus'** *backpack – and takes out the rabbit. She tucks it in beside him – then quietly leaves.* **Telemachus** *wakes.*

Telemachus   Where am I? Home? Or – wait –

He climbs out of bed and blinks, examining his surroundings.

Telemachus   This isn't my home. This isn't my room.

From the doorway comes a growl. **Telemachus** *turns in fear.*

Telemachus   And that –

The growl gets louder. A **Wild Beast** *enters, snarling at* **Telemachus**.

Telemachus   Is not my dog.

A second **Wild Beast** *enters. Together, they circle* **Telemachus**.

Telemachus   Good doggy. Is this your house? Do you want me to leave? I think that's probably a good idea –

He tries to leave, but the **Wild Beasts** *block his path.*

Telemachus   I don't have anything to give you, sorry –

The first **Wild Beast** *cocks its head – indicating the fluffy rabbit.*

Telemachus   Roger? No. He's mine. And he's special.

But the **Wild Beasts** *are un-persuaded.* **Telemachus** *hesitates, then:*

Telemachus   Fine – take him. What do I need a fluffy rabbit for anyway? I'm not a kid anymore.

He throws the rabbit to the **Wild Beasts** *– they howl in delight, shaking the rabbit in their jaws.* **Circe** *enters, carrying a tray of breakfast.*

Circe   Drop it! Drop that rabbit at once!

The **Wild Beasts** *obediently spit the rabbit out –* **Circe** *picks it up.*

Circe   This is yours, I think.

She offers the rabbit to **Telemachus**. *He reaches for it – then recoils.*

Circe   You're right – I'll wash it first. Sorry about them – I've tried to train them, but beasts will be beasts.

Telemachus   You live with wild animals?

Circe   Those two wouldn't survive a day in the wild.

Telemachus   They were born here?

Circe   They were born men – I turned them into beasts.

Telemachus   You turn men into beasts? Are you a witch?

Circe   I prefer 'enchantress'. And I only do it if the men behave like animals. Here – breakfast.

She offers **Telemachus** *the tray of food. He hesitates.*

Telemachus   Are you going to turn me into a beast?

Circe   If I was, why would I make you breakfast?

Telemachus *eats hungrily, as the* **Wild Beasts** *beg for scraps.*

Telemachus   Thanks for this. And for letting me stay.

Circe   Of course – thank you for staying. It can get lonely here, with only those two for company.

Telemachus   You don't have children? But – this room –

Circe   I thought I might, one day. I never did.

Telemachus   Why not? Because all men are beasts?

Circe   Not all of them – maybe just the ones I knew.

Telemachus   But you've got magic powers – can't you magic up whatever you want?

Circe   It doesn't really work like that –

Telemachus   But you can make things happen? Big things?

Circe   You don't need magic powers to make big things happen. But yes, I can make some things happen – why? Is there something you need?

Telemachus *hesitates – but remains silent.* **Circe** *presses, gently.*

Circe   You've come so far from home – what is it that you're looking for?

Telemachus   How do you know I'm looking for something?

Circe   Most people don't go on such a long journey, unless they're searching for something – or someone – very special.

Telemachus   I was looking for someone – for my dad. But I'm not sure I want to find him anymore. I'm not sure he wants to be found. I think that if he wanted to come home, he would have come home already.

Circe   Maybe he wants to, but he can't –

Telemachus   But parents can do anything they want.

Circe   No one can do everything they want – not beasts, not witches, not even parents.

Telemachus   Not me. I really thought I'd find my dad –

Circe   Maybe you will. Maybe you just need help –

Telemachus   And you can help?

Circe   I think I know someone who can. Tiresias, the prophet. They say he can answer any question. The problem is – he's in the underworld –

Telemachus   He's dead?

Circe   Not dead – immortal.

Telemachus   So why does he live down there?

Circe   I don't know. But you can ask him when you meet him –

Telemachus   I don't want to go to the underworld –

Circe   But you want to find your dad, don't you?

Telemachus   I – do.

Circe   So – go. You'll have to be brave.

Telemachus   I'm not sure I am brave –

Circe   If you weren't, you wouldn't have got this far.

She holds out **Telemachus'** *backpack. He puts it on – then hugs her.*

Telemachus   You'll be okay?

Circe   I have my wild beasts for company –

Telemachus   They'll be enough?

Circe   I'll have to be brave.

Telemachus *exits, as* **Circe** *watches him go.*

Seven: The Underworld

The underworld. Two **Guards** *man an elevator door. As* **Telemachus** *approaches, the* **First Guard** *puts a hand out to stop him.*

First Guard   ID, please.

Telemachus   ID? You need to know my age?

Second Guard   We don't care about your age – we need proof of when you died. So please – ID.

Telemachus   But I don't have ID –

First Guard   Because you're not dead?

Telemachus   No. I just – left it at home –

Second Guard   Don't waste our time – you're not the first one who's tried sneaking in without ID.

First Guard   You kids want to grow up so fast. I say – enjoy life while you have it. No need to come down here.

Telemachus   But I do need to come down here. I need to see Tiresias – I have a question for him.

Second Guard   He's the one who knows all things – everyone's got a question for him.

Telemachus   How come he's allowed in here? He's not dead.

First Guard   He's not – but he's immortal.

Telemachus   Maybe I'm immortal too.

Second Guard   How can you prove it?

Telemachus   I'm not dead, am I?

The **Guards** *hesitate, unsure. The* **Second Guard** *turns to the* **First Guard**.

First Guard   I don't see how we'd prove he's not immortal –

Second Guard   Not without potentially killing him, anyway.

The **Guards** *hesitate – then reluctantly step aside. The elevator doors open –* **Telemachus** *takes a deep breath, then enters. The doors close behind him. When they open again, the space is hazy, full of dancing bodies. Music pulses through the space. Hands reach for* **Telemachus** *– he pushes them away. The crowd thins and the music fades – until the only sound is the faint beeping of machines and raspy breathing. A voice calls out:*

Tiresias   Who's there?

A faint light on **Tiresias***, seated and elderly, knees covered with a blanket.*

Telemachus   Are you – Tiresias?

Tiresias   Not what you expected? Or not what you expected to find here?

Telemachus   You're –

Tiresias   Old? You can say it. That's the thing about being immortal – you live forever but it doesn't mean you get to stay young. Not young like you, anyway.

Telemachus   I'm not that young.

Tiresias   You might not feel it, but you are – compared to me, at least. So tell me, child – what brings you here?

Telemachus   I thought you could answer every question –

Tiresias   I can – but it still helps to hear it from you.

Telemachus   I'm looking for my dad –

Tiresias   I can't hear you – an eternity in the underworld will damage anyone's hearing. Come closer.

Telemachus   I – don't want to.

Tiresias   Why not?

Telemachus   Because – I'm scared.

Tiresias   I don't blame you – but I need you to come closer.

Telemachus *hesitates – then approaches.*

Tiresias   Now give your old Tiresias a kiss on the cheek –

Telemachus   Really?

Tiresias   I'm joking. So – you're looking for your dad.

Telemachus   You'll tell me where he is?

Tiresias   I'll try. But first – you tell me what you know.

Telemachus   His name's Odysseus – from Ithaca. He left when I was young – I don't remember much. But people say he's brave and strong – a hero. Though –

Tiresias   Go on –

Telemachus   I'm not so sure he is a hero. Or that he's the man that I set out to find. He's – hurt people. Tricked them. Burned their cities to the ground. A woman told me that she fell in love with him –

Tiresias   And is that bad?

Telemachus   Yes – when that woman's not my mum.

Tiresias   Sounds like you have a lot to talk about – so we'd best find him so you two can chat. You don't have anything of his? To help me find him in my mind?

Telemachus   I have – this.

He reaches into the backpack – and takes out the photo.

Tiresias   That's him, is it? And you, as a baby?

Telemachus   Yes – will it help you?

Tiresias   Let me see –

He takes the photo. He closes his eyes – then opens them again.

I saw the two of you together. You in his arms, just like the photograph. But you're the age that you are now – and he's much older than he was.

Telemachus   What does that mean?

Tiresias   It means that's in your future – yours and his.

Telemachus   So I do find him?

Tiresias   Yes –

Telemachus   But you can't tell me how?

Tiresias   If I could tell you everything, there would be nothing to discover. And if there was nothing to discover, then it would be a long and lonely life.

Telemachus   When you see us, what else do you see?

Tiresias   You speak to him. You ask him –

Telemachus   What? What do I ask?

Tiresias   What do you think you ask?

Telemachus   I think – I ask him why he left. And didn't come back for such a long time. And whether there was anything I could have done to make him stay.

Tiresias   It doesn't take the gift of sight to answer that. You were a baby when he left – there's nothing that you could have done. Whatever happened, none of it's your fault.

Telemachus   But what do I do now?

Tiresias   You go back to the surface – to the living. And you promise me something –

Telemachus   Yes?

Tiresias   You won't come back here for a really really really long time. And one more thing – your photograph.

He hands **Telemachus** *the photo. He takes it and* **Tiresias** *turns away. Music begins. Alone,* **Telemachus** *sings.*

Telemachus
> He said that I would find you, Dad,
> He said that he was sure.
> Yet here I am with just a photo –
> And an open door.

Eight: Penelope

Ithaca. Music begins. **Penelope** – *sewing discarded beside her –
sings.*

Penelope
> So many times I've thought I heard
> His footsteps at the door.
> Yet here I am, without the one,
> That I am waiting for.
>
> Where are you now – my boy, my love, my child?
> You've never been so far away from home.
> I wait for you here, awake and dreamless,
> It's hard to sleep when your baby is gone.
>
> And the days go past and they turn to weeks,
> And every hour feels like ten.
> Alone I wonder where my boy is,
> And when he'll be home again.

A sound at the door – **Penelope** *rushes to open it. The* **Ithacans**
enter.

First Ithacan   Penelope!

Penelope   You're home –

Second Ithacan   We are!

Penelope   And Telemachus –

First Ithacan   Telemachus?

Penelope   Is he – not with you –

Second Ithacan   We thought he was with you?

Penelope   Why would you think he was with me? He was with you –

First Ithacan   He was, but then –

Penelope   But then –

The **Second Ithacan** *replies quietly, almost inaudibly.*

Second Ithacan   He jumped into the sea.

Penelope   He – what?

The **Second Ithacan** *replies, louder this time.*

Second Ithacan   He jumped into the sea.

Penelope   He – what –

She stumbles backwards, shocked. The **Second Ithacan** *shouts:*

Second Ithacan   He jumped into the sea!

The **First Ithacan** *catches* **Penelope***, steadying her.*

First Ithacan   I think she heard you.

Second Ithacan   Okay – I just wasn't sure –

Penelope   I heard you – but I can't believe it's true. You let my child jump into the sea –

First Ithacan   We didn't let him –

Second Ithacan   Couldn't stop him –

First Ithacan   You know what he's like.

Penelope   I do –

First Ithacan   We searched for him and then we thought –

Second Ithacan   He must be here!

First Ithacan   He's smart, he's brave – he must have found his own way home!

Second Ithacan   But – he's not home –

Penelope   He isn't, no.

Second Ithacan   So then he's –

A moment. **Penelope** *stares at the* **Ithacans***, desperate. Then:*

First Ithacan   We don't know. And we're – so sorry –

Penelope   No – it's not your fault –

Second Ithacan   It is – we let him go –

Penelope   You didn't let him go – I did. He's my son – and I let him go. And now he's lost. And it's my fault.

First Ithacan   It's not your fault –

Penelope   It is. I was supposed to keep him safe. And I – I –

She stops, overcome. The **Ithacans** *hold her. A moment, then:*

Second Ithacan   Maybe we can blame Odysseus? Not like he's here to defend himself –

Penelope *laughs, despite herself – then straightens, urgent now.*

Penelope   I've got to go – to find him –

First Ithacan   No – we'll go –

Penelope   But I'm his mother – it's my job –

First Ithacan   And you can't do it all alone.

Second Ithacan   We'll find your son, Penelope – we will.

Penelope   But –

First Ithacan   You stay here – you have your own work to do.

Second Ithacan   That wedding dress won't undo itself.

Penelope   So I just stay here – sewing every day and then undoing what I've done? Until –

First Ithacan   We come back with your son. We will.

Penelope   How do you know?

Second Ithacan   Because we won't give up.

Penelope   That's what I said to him. To Telemachus – in the letter that I wrote. Just don't give up.

First Ithacan   I'm sure he won't. So don't you give up either.

The **Ithacans** *pick up their swords and exit.* **Penelope***, determined now, returns to her sewing – decisively undoing her work. As she does, she sings:*

Penelope
I can't give up, I must believe,
I'll see my son again.
My Telemachus will return –
The question now is – when?

Nine: The Sea Monster

Telemachus *sits alone, despondent, on the shore. The* **Ithacans** *enter.*

Second Ithacan   Telemachus! We found you –

First Ithacan   I'm so glad we found you –

Second Ithacan   And so glad that you're okay.

The **Ithacans** *embrace* **Telemachus** *– but he doesn't respond.*

Second Ithacan   Are you okay? You seem sort of – not okay?

Telemachus   I'm fine. I'm just – tired. It's been a long journey.

First Ithacan   So – rest. We can keep going in the morning –

Telemachus   Keep going where? How am I meant to know which way to go? I went to see Tiresias –

Second Ithacan   In the underworld?

First Ithacan   Maybe let's not tell your mum about that.

Telemachus   He told me that I'd find my dad –

Second Ithacan   That's great!

Telemachus   But couldn't tell me where or how.

Second Ithacan   That's – not so helpful –

Telemachus   Since then I've been sitting here – I don't know how long. But I don't know where else to go.

First Ithacan   Maybe – it's time to go home.

Telemachus   I can't – I haven't found my dad –

Second Ithacan   But you will – that's what the prophet said.

Music begins. **Penelope**'s *voice is heard – a call to* **Telemachus***:*

Penelope
　The most important thing is to return,
　My son, my heart, my bones, my world.

The **Ithacans** *set sail with* **Telemachus***. As they journey, they sing.*

Ithacans
　There comes a time when you must turn
　And face the way you came.
　In Ithaca your mother waits
　To see her son again.

　The sea is calm, the sky is clear,
　There's nothing blocks our way.
　And so we speed our little boat
　To Ithaca again.

　We travel onward, homeward bound,
　Us brave adventurers three.
　But what's that rising from the deep –

Scylla – *a six-headed sea monster – rises from the ocean. In horror:*

Telemachus   A monster of the sea!

Scylla   Who are you calling a monster?

The music rises, as **Scylla** *thrashes the water. She sings.*

Scylla
So many men like to call you a monster,
The moment that you scream or yell.
But what is the problem with being a monster,
I've never been able to tell.

A monster is big! A monster is strong!
A monster stops you in your tracks!
I promise once you meet a monster,
There's no going back.

So many men like to think of a monster,
As something that they have to fix –
No need for stressing, to me it's a blessing,
Why have one head when you could have six?

Scylla *reaches into the boat and grasps* **Telemachus** *in a tentacle, lifting him into the air. He screams, as she lifts him to her mouth.*

Scylla
There's no better life than the life of a monster,
And to be a sea monster, at that –
Relax everyday, and then lunch comes my way,
Just sun, sea, sand – and free snacks!

First Ithacan   Quick – maybe there's some way to distract her –

The **Ithacans** *desperately search* **Telemachus'** *backpack.*

Second Ithacan   There's nothing. Just – a letter. But it says 'don't open, until you really need to'.

First Ithacan   I think we really need to now! Telemachus, catch!

The **First Ithacan** *throws the letter to* **Telemachus** *– as he catches it, the space dims around him. All that remains visible are the faces* *of* **Penelope** – **Scylla***'s six heads in darkness above her* – *and* **Telemachus**.

Penelope   Telemachus. I'm going to say something adults don't say enough to children – you're right. I can't make you stay in Ithaca – you're my baby, but you're not a kid anymore. If you're determined to go, I'll let you – but I'll still do everything I can to keep you safe. I'm not a fighter like your father – but I know there are many ways to win a war. The most important thing is – don't give up. Even when things seem impossible, keep going –

Telemachus   But I've already come so far –

Penelope   That's life, kid – it's a really really really long journey. But I'll see you soon – just don't give up.

A roar of water, as lights rise on **Scylla** *again.* **Telemachus** *struggles – then strikes her with his sword. Her six heads fall away – as the boat lurches, reaching land. Ithaca.*

First Ithacan   Ithaca! We're home!

Second Ithacan   Race you to the front door –

First Ithacan   Come on, Telemachus!

Telemachus   You go ahead – there's something I need to do.

Second Ithacan   Okay –

Telemachus   By myself.

Second Ithacan   Okay.

The **Ithacans** *exit.* **Telemachus** *faces the sea, still clutching his sword.*

Telemachus   Dad. I hoped I'd get to say this to your face – and maybe I still will. But in case I don't – I'm sorry. That I couldn't find you. And I'm sorry you left. You missed a lot – and we missed you a lot. I spent a lifetime, waiting for you to return – and another lifetime searching for you. But I've followed in your footsteps far enough – it's time to take a different path. It's time for me to go home.

He throws his sword into the sea. Music begins. He sings.

Telemachus
I set off, Dad, from Ithaca
And sailed across to Troy.
Where you had gone to fight a war,
When I was just a boy.

In Troy we found a city sacked,
They said it was your work.
I couldn't make myself believe,
That you could cause such hurt.

From there went to the cyclops' den,
He tried to capture me.
Was helped out by two talking sheep,
Before I was his tea.

Next travelled to an island,
So full of fruited trees.
Was told that just a single bite,
Would wipe your memory.

Calypso said you ate that fruit,
Yet kept your thoughts of home.
But still for all those many years,
Left Mum and me alone.

I crossed the waves by magic wind,
And heard my mother's song,
I swam until I almost drowned,
But never found my mum.

My journey took me downwards,
To the underworld below.
I met a man who said he knew,
All that there was to know.

He said that I would find you, Dad,
He said that he was sure.
Yet here I am, returned without
What I was looking for.

He hangs his head. **Penelope** *enters, rushing to embrace him.*

Ten: Home

Penelope and **Telemachus** *hug – it is long and heartfelt. Then:*

Penelope   That sounds like a really really really long journey.

Telemachus   It really really was.

Penelope   I'm proud of you. I really really am.

She embraces **Telemachus** *again – but he pulls away.*

Telemachus   But I failed, Mum – I couldn't do what I set out to do. I couldn't find Dad. I went a long way and got lost and scared and tired and came home.

Penelope   I'm glad you did.

Telemachus   You're not angry with me?

Penelope   Why would I be angry?

Telemachus   Because I didn't listen – you told me not to go, but I did. You said I wouldn't find Dad and I didn't.

Penelope   So why did you go?

Telemachus   Because I wanted to find him. And I wanted to prove myself. And I wanted to have an adventure.

Penelope   And you had an adventure. And you proved yourself –

Telemachus   But I didn't find Dad.

Penelope   Telemachus, he's a grown-up. He can make his own way home.

Telemachus   But he hasn't, has he?

Penelope *smiles, sadly. A short silence, then:*

Telemachus   I had this really clear idea of Dad – but the closer I got to finding him, the harder it became to keep that person in my head. He started to turn into –

Penelope   A real person?

Telemachus   Yeah. But not just real –

Penelope   Fallible?

Telemachus   What does fallible mean?

Penelope   Someone who makes mistakes. Who's not always a hero. Who doesn't always do the right thing or the good thing or the kind thing, all the time –

Telemachus   I didn't think that Dad could be unkind –

Penelope   Your dad can be a lot of things – everyone can, but especially your dad. He's a complicated man.

Telemachus   Do you think he'll ever come home?

Penelope   I don't know.

Telemachus   Thank you.

Penelope   For what?

Telemachus   For saying you don't know.

Penelope   Thank you.

Telemachus   For what?

Penelope   For coming home. And for being brave enough to leave in the first place.

Telemachus   Maybe next time I'll follow in your footsteps, Mum.

Penelope   Maybe next time I'll follow in yours.

She and **Telemachus** *hug. The* **Ithacans** *enter. Music begins.*

Ithacans
It ends – like many stories – with return.
A son who makes his way back home.
He finds his mother waiting –
And she sees how much he's grown.

Telemachus

It ends – with a change.
A child now more man than boy.
But in some ways he's still the same,
As when he left his home for Troy.

Ithacans

Ten years, ten years –

Penelope

The sea is calm and the sky is clear,
Now that my son is back – he's here.
This empty cave becomes our home again –
And no more lonely nights for me to fear.

Ithacans

Without you, without you –

Telemachus

I've been following my father,
Now the next steps are for me.
It's time for me to take some time,
To find out who I want to be.

Ithacans

It's a really really really long journey,
So long they call it an odyssey –
Across the land, across the water,
And we're still home in time for tea.

Penelope

It's been a really really really long journey,
Now my son's come back to me –

Telemachus

Across the land, across the water,
And now I'm home –

All

An odyssey.

Ithacans
Telemachus has returned!

Penelope
My son, my heart, my bones, my world,
My love, my child, my joy.
And the song goes –

The song continues, as they dance together. It reaches a crescendo:

All
The Odyssey!

Then – the doorbell rings. Blackout.